S0-BOT-925

Bread Crumbs

BREAD CRUMBS

Poems

Cynthia Tremblay

Lynx House Press
Spokane, Washington

Acknowledgements

The poems "Brownstone," "Waiting," "Life at Thirteen, a Dream at 33," "Tahiti," "Drought Summer (1971)," "Bitter Wells, Colorado," "Song of a Woman Alone Before Her Child Is Born," "Letter," "Jack Poem," "Morning News," "What I Do," "For the Geese," "In Exactly Twelve Years...," and "Laserium" all appeared in *Morning News*, Lynx House Press, 1976, and are reprinted by permission.

"Suggestions from a Fall Garden," "Song of a Woman Before Her Child Is Born," "What I Do," and "Or" were performed through the High Plains Arts Center (Ft. Collins, CO). The poem "Or" was part of an integrated arts performance, "The peripheral Visions of Three Women," performed in 1993, also through the High Plains Arts Center.

The poem "Or" is inspired by the watercolor painting "A Multitude of Arks" by Jon E. Kutzik, Emeritus Professor of Art, Colorado State University; and the painting itself was inspired by Dylan Thomas' poem "A Multitude of Arks."

Copyright © 2020 by Cynthia Tremblay
ISBN 978-0-89924-170-8
Design by Kristina Pfleegor
Author Photo by Jared Charney
Cover Art by Evan Howell

These poems are inspired and/or encouraged by my family, past and present, the Charney family, Lorrie, Sue, John C., Jim Scrim, Chrissy, Carol (who listens), Iruka, Sarah, Jo, Gay, and Rosey (who saves things).

Thanks also to the editorial kindness and patience of Christopher Howell.

Contents

Poetry is a life-cherishing force. For poems are not words, after all,
But fires for the cold, ropes let down to the lost, something as
Necessary as bread in the pockets of the hungry.

—Mary Oliver

1948

Red barns with sharp roofs
let snow slide off.
New green pushes promises up
from pasture swamps.
Dooryard trees believe
leaves will come.
The road curves
to the next farm. I see the way
a kid would go: cross lots, straight
over the hill.

Order

Grace talks to plants, house and garden, urging them
    to grow. They do. Begonias
all winter, then portulacas, nasturtiums, chrysanthe
    mums blaze their gypsy flames.

In July, Grace takes the small hand sickle, walks down
    the wooden porch stairs and
resolutely and methodically slices tiger lily stems, still
    beautiful as they fall into neat
rows on the ground.

The child, playing nearby, who loves them for their
    orangeness, asks, "Why?"
meaning why cheer them on only to cut them down?
    Grace says only, "They spread,
take over everything." To the child this answer makes
    no sense. She thinks it would
be wonderful if all the world were covered with orange
    lilies.

She won't know for years they need to rein things in, to
    control what can be controlled,
to salvage a bit of order in an overwhelmed life, things
    that spread, that take over
everything.

As the child watches, Grace's right hand twists the sickle,
     her unspoken thoughts
perhaps also twisting, as she continues to cut the stalks,
     fallen in rows of orange
haze.

Grace straightens up, and smiles at her granddaughter,
     takes her hand and they walk
together up the stairs.

Rosebush and Snake Smoke

Once again a small tanned girl
in sunsuit and floppy galoshes
descends porch stairs into Saturday
where her father practices golf
under the apple tree.
Her boot buckles lock.
She tumbles into the rose bush, yelling.
Her father looks up from his ball, sees
a small snake crawl near his daughter.

Once again the girl does not feel
the thorns in her bleeding legs so much
as wonder, as does her mother,
running from the house, why
the golf club crashes, bits of snake
flying perfumed by
crushed roses.

Once again her father,
weekend ruined, stands
by the rubbish barrel burning
small dragon remains like St. George
ruing that he sees the world awry,
unable to tell a snake from a rosebush,
unable to protect her.
Once again as snake smoke rises
her rose-thorn scratches
become mercurochrome blossoms.

May 1956

A certain numbness warns me not to look
at the other caps and gowns as they float away
toward their futures. A certain numbness
holds me in a place
that has no known center.

Formerly dubbed "Smart Girl" in my childhood world,
I am dissolving. By day, I turn my collar up, so I'll look...
I don't care, whatever it is. No one knew about multiple
intelligences.

By night, lilac intoxication of cool spring
holds a promise of something beyond the closing door,
the numbed blank and empty acceptance of mediocrity.
Cool lilac blossoms touch my cheek.
Serious moonlight is my consolation.

Brownstone

The landlady was believed
to be a witch. One woman
wore a bathing cap and suit
for washing dishes in the shower.
The man down the hall
coughed so loud doors could not
hide him from bill collectors.
My roommate was in the middle
of a five-year engagement
to a man in a different state
and I was in the middle
of the night playing Bessie Smith.

I expected no deliverance from this place
and carried it in my head on a brown shelf.
Years later I dared to look. Someone
had painted the whole thing orange.

Waiting

Waiting with a green bottle
to numb midnight if still alone.
My landlord the driveway ascending
from New Year's Eve to God knows what reality
of New Year's Day. From my window I see him
and his peaked pink paper hat.
Why must I keep waiting for someone
to say "I love you," or at least
some words that would make a difference.
It's such a drag to wait for Superman.
Sometime I am going to put on my cape
and fly out the window.

Life at Thirteen, a Dream at 33

Looking to lipstick for definition,
I stood before the perfumed sanctuary.
Hushed by thick carpet, swaddled in cologne,
transfixed by the soft-voiced clerk
who assured me that #10 was "right,"
that the application of this or that powder
to this or that cheek
would make me look like a woman.

In my dream a young man wore eye make-up,
heavy black ovals with red ochre-filled corners.
My hair was long and plain,
my feet were bare. I wore my old brown dress.
His Egyptian gaze slid toward me.
I shifted my weight to my heels and sped to the ceiling.
I bounced lightly down in a corner of a cabin.
He turned to focus on me again.
I bounded to the ceiling.
Rooted to room's dead center he revolved,
a sinister low-speed turntable doll.
I bounded again and again, just out of reach of those eyes.
My terror expanded to strength.
I exploded the cabin, invisibly and soundlessly.

When I looked back,
it was there, settling, atom by atom,
but I, outside, welcomed with sky,
smiles, flowers, my own incredible eyes.

Keeping It Together

In the corner where we always slept in those summers of
    the army tent,
the foam rubber mattress on the wooden platform, the
    fragrant forest
mingled with wild blueberries. The world had been way
    too much with us,
and we stepped aside, hoping for perspective. Terrified by
    Kent State,
and the knowledge that there was no way to avoid the
    echoes of war,
we nonetheless had to try. Taking our boys, four and six,
    from relative
comfort, Dad a year-round teaching job, stay-at-home
    Mom, and grandparents
nearby, to live in the woods was frightening. Bill and I
    could not see a clear
future.

One summer Bill worked as a maintenance man for the
    Amherst School District,
coming back to the campsite evenings exhausted. One
    summer I worked in a
pickle factory, shoes and feet stained with running streams
    of vinegar and spice.
We saw some beautiful days. Ben, who was four, had just
    outgrown effects of

a two-years-long milk allergy, which had not been
    properly diagnosed, leaving
him thin and pale. The first summer in the woods saw a
    transformation.
Learning to swim in the nearby lake in the long days, pale
    skin turning golden,
Ben sang and spoke poetry.

Billy, always observant and aware, felt the risk in this
    adventure. He, too,
loved the lake, and swam every day. He was helpful and
    brave, always,
but lying in his corner on his foam mattress, he must have
    wondered what
lay ahead. Maybe he could sense our desire to keep our
    family together,
even under precarious circumstances, and together make it
    through
this tunnel of uncertainty. We all have the memory of
    campfire smoke,
Massachusetts woods and sun-simmered lake ripples,
    those summers.

Song of a Woman Alone before Her Child Is Born

What can I give you
in this bitter world
where dogs die and people
get where they're going?

Only the earth, which
is not mine to give—this
dandelion, these roots going
into the earth, the roots of
next year and next.

Jack Poem

Whirlwind
nightwind
inside and out
the window

your dad holds your hands
and swings you out
and around
your brothers whirling in their own orbits.

Your dad swaying
the trees swaying o Jack
will you remember
the whirlwind night
I watched out the window
as the wind rose

what center holds you to us,
to yourself?

Laserium

Images…generated by a single one-watt
krypton gas laser, displaying the purest
colors ever devised or seen by man.

Red clouds stretch to spider webs, unwind
to dancers, a handful of dry spaghetti
finishes a drum solo and fans out to mushroom spores.
Gyres sing my lullaby. I doze as huge red circles
swallow me up and spit me out.
Bill squeezes my arm to see if I know it was the Gyres.
I wake up. Jack's sleeping face floats white
in the darkness. Maybe God thinks
we're ready for this. Scientists dance
with the vision that drove Van Gogh mad.

In Exactly Twelve Years the Parks and Recreation Department Will Consider Me a Senior Citizen So It's Time to Count My Blessings

The blessing of the breasts took place when my first baby
    nursed there.
The blessing of the other womanly parts took place
    with whatever free loving there has been.

The blessing of the eyes took place when they looked inward
    and did not turn away.
The blessing of the hands took place when I was at last
    able to feel compassion for them, nail-bitten,
    guilt-ridden effigies of my childhood failures.

My legs are furthest from grace, for they alone have suffered
    vanity.
As yet no formula is known for the blessing of the legs.

Tahiti

When we get off the ship
I will sit down
and look at the sea.
You will search for a tavern
and drinking friends.
I will write poems about taverns.
You will write astonishing poems
about the sea.

Bitter Wells, Colorado

At noon I run to the mailbox
hoping for news good enough to bring you home.
The news comes in the evening.
A phone-call from a bar tells me you're drowning
In bitter wells.
My last illusion sinks with the sun.

This morning you said
"I'd rather talk to you than anyone."
All I can hope to share is the empty night.

Not wanting to wake the children
I contain a scream, silently pound walls.

Drought Summer (1971)

for Nick

You told me around Carmel or Monterrey
the geraniums grow huge, their roots in the ocean.
You gave me French Marigolds in a plastic tray,
their gold surviving all catastrophes through August.
You knew the only way to fight whiskey was flowers.
Now I say two words I couldn't then, "alcoholic,"
and "thanks."

Letter

When I finally understood
that you wanted to try life "on its own"
without the drinking thing, I felt
as if you had picked up and bodily thrown out
some third presence that had always been with us,
eating with us, sleeping with us,
taking baths with us, pushing between us.

This is the liberation I have longed for:
to see you as you are, to hear your own voice speak,
and to be seen and heard the same.

Or (From a Painting)

Perhaps she can float and he can't. Perhaps he will be tragically lonely after she drifts away. He will be heavy with the blue of loneliness and the empty hands of loneliness. Perhaps she will float with the tipsy wonder of jade and carnelian, her head growing more orange, her shoulders violet, her elbows more indigo and her belly green, green and inseparable from the boat growing green and indigo and violet and trailing fiery lilies. Perhaps at that white pinwheel of no return she will try to float back to the other, noticing for the first time his spine of gold and that he too trails lilies of fire.

Or

Perhaps he can float and she can't. Perhaps she will be tragically lonely after he drifts away. She will be heavy with the blue of loneliness and the empty hands of loneliness. Perhaps he will float with the tipsy wonder of jade and carnelian, his head growing more orange, his shoulders violet, his elbows more indigo and his belly green and inseparable from the boat growing green and indigo and violet and trailing fiery lilies. Perhaps at that white pinwheel of no return he will try to float back to the other, noticing for the first time her spine of gold and that she too trails lilies of fire.

Suggestions from a Fall Garden

What if we were aesthetic creatures first? What if before
the meat hunger and the seed hunger and even before thirst
we were nourished by what met our eyes? Swiss chard
    leaves
huge as the pharaoh's fan. Summer squash as if varnished,
grainy, past eating. Dill heads, brown lace tangled with vines,
and mingling at will with weeds, exempt at this season
from the gardener's customary "edible/non-edible"
    distinctions.
Perhaps to notice the grace of dried grass, to give symmetry
of thistle its due, is to reach back to a time when our senses
weren't so sure of themselves and survival was a million
years from definition.

Morning News

An aluminum-bodied trailer truck
with a green cab
ran over the sun.
The sun didn't care,
it rose, unflattened, without tire marks,
over Riverside Avenue.

Ellen's Chowdah

Glacial butter glides
Through thick cream and North Shore clams—
Ocean in a bowl.

Dickinson

She's the cool water we crave,
with just enough New England spice.
She's nutmeg and cloves and a bit

of black pepper so we know
she's for real and so, so earnest.

When the whimsy starts to rise
on butterfly wings—
look out!

What I Do

In average traffic, I hold my stop sign
like a badminton racquet, in heavy traffic,
high, like a butterfly net.
When there's no traffic, I hold it
like five dozen long-stemmed American Beauty roses,
I having just won the Miss America Pageant.
During a blizzard we become a haiku, the red sign
against my cheek. "STOP" to the wind.

Once I imagined holding the sign high enough
to stop a line of Canada geese, just for a moment,
so that two crows might cross.

For the Geese

In September I stand on the corner of Stuart and Welch.
The Canada geese fly southward, their voices
eerie bulb horn music in the early air.

On a hot day in May one goose quickly crosses the airway,
not wanting to burn his wings on the sizzling sky.

They don't always fly. On the ground they become huge,
substantial like dogs, or people. I've seen them,
one or two immense birds
hitch-hiking beside the road.

Moths

A row of them
hide from sunlight,
wings folded, behind
a curtain.
Tiny dusty fangless
vampires,
we wish them gone.
Yet one inspires awe,
even pity.
Trapped on the birdbath surface
Ophelia's gauzy garments
outstretch.

Walking to the Mailbox

(Written in 1989)

This is not about resemblance,
but rather, about attitude: this is knowing
how it feels to be the one
surviving, walking with a scarf
into the weather—taking care
of whatever needs care.

In this snow swirl
at the end of March
I become my mother
in 1950, babushka ties
whipped back over wool coat collar,
walking, perhaps,
to the clothesline,
finding shirts
stiff with flakes.

My real mother
heads toward Florida
in a Ford, a chiffon scarf
rests lightly on her neat white hair.
At this moment, and I am glad for her,
of the two of us
she is the younger.

From the Cave of Sleep

I think,
waking from
dreamy speculations,
such as
which is more beautiful—
a bird's song or a flute which sounds
like a bird's song—
it's pleasant, this near
dream state
where possibilities float.
My mother, at ninety,
on waking, lying in her bed,
said one early morning,
"I could be a teenager,
just jump up and do things,
until I try to move."

Black & White Photo in Central Park

Among the tall trees
the boy is seated on a wolf,
a cast metal wolf. Bronze fur
rises in sharp ridges.
The wolf is high; the boy is not sure
about this. What sustains him
in this frozen moment is
he knows his dad is there

standing near the base
of the statue. His eyes look
at the camera, but his heart looks
at the boy

seated on the high wolf. What
allows this enchantment is
he knows the spell
will soon be broken,
that he will lift his son down,
and they will move from the dark
woods into familiar day.
The camera clicks.

The Mechanical Horse at King Sooper's

No one begs for coins
The horse has no motion now
Grandkids move away

Renovation

1.

Cover a broken life
with lattice.
It is a quick and cheap fix.

2.

Paint it the color of
happiness. If that is not
available, choose
the closest match.
No one will know
but you.

Leaving October

This season of golden days
is hard in the turning
toward somber November.

There is another season,
internal, yet harder
in the turning.

Optimism's bright shawl
becomes
regret's charcoal cloak.

October Again

Ash leaves fall
one by one.
Foothills darken
under this ombre sky.
Crickets, geese,
trains sound
away
and soft.
Dusk
neutralizes gold. Only
memory's brightness
holds.

October III

Ash towers
march down the ditch;
gold trees upstage
deep blue foothills;
cloud sculptures float.

Today's horoscope announces
"Hope is an essential ingredient
of any good plan."
Nature's grand procession promotes
this possibility.

No Computer Today

for Grace

No computer today,
no online streaming melody,
no buttons to push.

I will have to light a candle
on my windowsill, imagine music
of flame.

I will have only ordinary miracles today,
light and water and memory
of the nearly forgotten.

We are people for whom
a newly-observed bird, or star,
can make
all the difference.

For My Boys

Facing life's puzzle,
I follow the breadcrumb path
through misty spring woods.

In your young years my clouds
of anxiety engulfed you daily
like second-hand smoke.
Our lives were made of it,
my bewildering limits.

Who scattered the breadcrumbs?
There must be careful
stepping.

This is not to say
we did not laugh or feel joy,
laughing sometimes even
knowing the driver of the car
did not know east from west,
left from right.

The lovely experiences, the great
moments, however, could not
erase the backdrop of our anxious
scene.

What is the breadcrumb path?
It is lifelong.
It needs a strong light
and is hard to follow with
a sense of direction that never
grew up.

Other people's clouds
even with lovely spring moments
and laughter
become a burden. I give thanks
that the second-hand cloud
drifted away from you
on a clear day.

The hummingbird's twitter
lifts this moment from sadness.
Bird, I say thank you.

Two Poems for Bill

1.

Because you refuse to be bound
by others' ideas of the possible
you brought the thin lost girl
I was into the light.
You have made books happen;
your words have moved people.
My delight is transitory, bound
by the possible—a hummingbird
at the feeder, a dish well-cooked
and quickly eaten. But
for your delight, I wish
the impossible—a utopian rosebush
where "blooms all summer" means
petals never fall from
any rose.

2.

After the snow
            …the sun
pouring in through glass
this morning,
after our familiar breakfast
while discussing

(arguing about) things like
whether or not Norman Rockwell's
illustrated world
still exists in New England
anywhere but in nostalgia,
I realize
all I ever hoped for was
talking to you
all my life.

Home Planet

Today on my
home planet
there are blue jays
and chickadees.
The sun warmth falls
softy on my face,
in January. A distant
windchime sounds
a call to worship.

Cynthia Tremblay grew up in North Brookfield, Massa-chusetts, and attended Clark University, in Worcester, Massachusetts, where she met and married the poet Bill Tremblay. Together they have three sons and since 1974 have lived in Ft. Collins, Colorado. Cynthia says of herself that she is at best a poet, at worst (when fog covers the foothills) a person who does not know east from west.